Workbook 4

Recipe for Reading

Connie Russo

EDUCATORS PUBLISHING SERVICE
Cambridge and Toronto

Acquisitions/Development: Bonnie Lass
Cover Design: Karen Lomigora
Cover Photo: Sharpe Shots Photography
Typesetting: Sarah Rakitin
Editor: Elissa Gershowitz
Managing Editor: Sheila Neylon

ISBN 978-0-8388-0494-0
Printed in U.S.A.
15 16 PPG 20 19 18

Contents

Lesson 43

-ed Ending

-ed is added to the end of a word to make a new word. The ending -ed says
> **/d/** as in yelled
> **/ĭd/** as in melted
> **/t/** as in brushed

Read each sentence. Underline the word with **-ed.** Circle the sound for **-ed** in that word.

The kids jumped up and down.   /d/   /id/   /t/

The class planted a bush.   /d/   /id/   /t/

A dog kissed Ted on the hand.   /d/   /id/   /t/

I missed the van.   /d/   /id/   /t/

A thrush landed on its nest.   /d/   /id/   /t/

The thrush filled the nest with eggs.   /d/   /id/   /t/

Add -ed to the underlined word to complete the sentence. Then read each question and answer.

Did Bill <u>act</u> glad? Yes, Bill _____

glad.

Did the hen <u>nest</u> in the box? Yes, the hen

_____ there.

Where did Dan <u>print</u> a p? He _____

a p in the blank.

Did Nell <u>spell</u> cat? She _____ cat.

How long did the tot <u>yell</u>? The tot

_____ all day.

Where did you <u>camp</u>? We _____

at the pond.

2

Read the sentence. Underline the word with -ed. Then write the root word.

The cat winked at us.

_____

The tot bumped into the bed.

_____

The sun lasted all day.

_____

What dented the trunk?

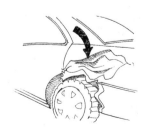

_____

Check off the sentence that matches the picture.

We camped at the pond.

We stomped up the hill.

The mom kissed the tot.

The mom yelled at the tot.

Jen blushed when Ted winked.

Jen blinked when Ted winked.

Pat filled the glass.

Tap on the glass.

A thrush tested its eggs.

A thrush nested on its eggs.

The man put on his pants.

The pup panted in the hot sun.

4

Read the story. Underline 7 words with the ending **-ed.** Then list 6 of them in the chart.

Camping

My dog Bud and I camped out. I put up a small tent. I went to bed. Bud rested next to me. Bud must have smelled something. He yanked at me. He wanted me to get up. A skunk had bumped into the tent. Bud and I dashed out of there fast!

Word	+	Ending	=	New Word
_____		**-ed**		_____
_____		**-ed**		_____
_____		**-ed**		_____
_____		**-ed**		_____
_____		**-ed**		_____
_____		**-ed**		_____

Lesson 44

Magic e in one-syllable words

Say the names of the pictures. Then circle the pictures whose names have the same vowel sound.

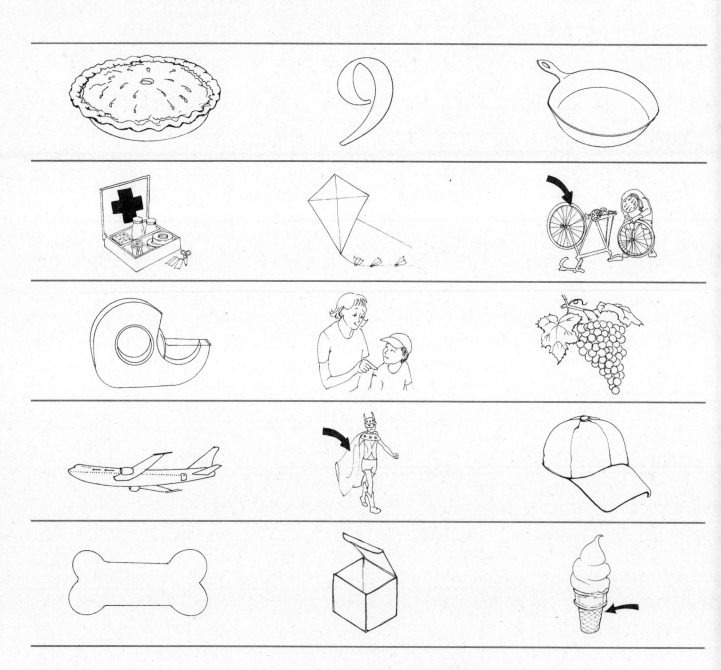

Say the names of all the pictures you circled. What is the same about the vowel sounds in all of these names?

Add a magic e to each word to create new words. Then read each sentence.

Add a magic e to pin and you get

_____ .

Add a magic e to tap and you get

_____ .

Add a magic e to cub and you get

_____ .

Add a magic e to cap and you get

_____ .

Add a magic e to kit and you get

_____ .

Read the word and circle the matching picture. Listen for the vowel that says its name.

skate

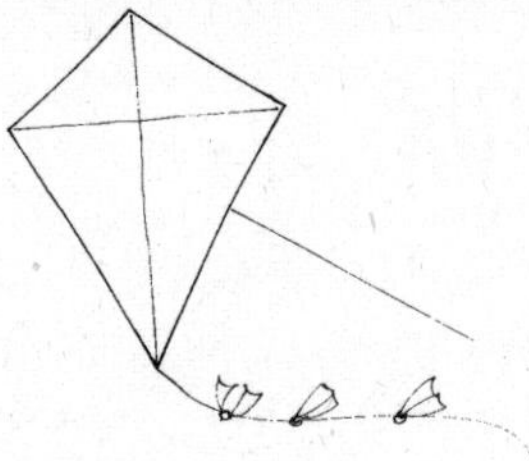

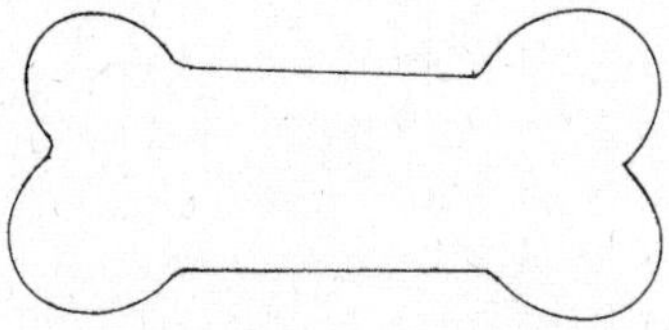

cone

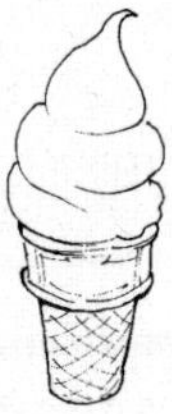

bike

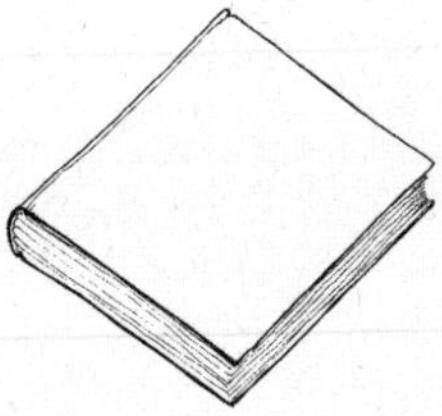

nine

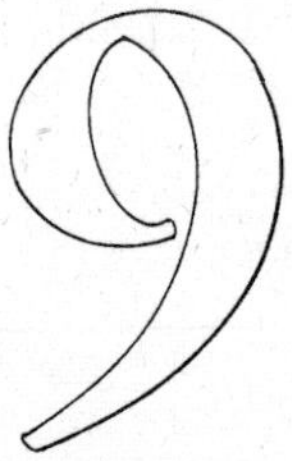

plane

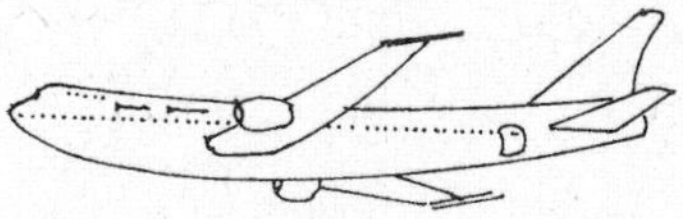

grape

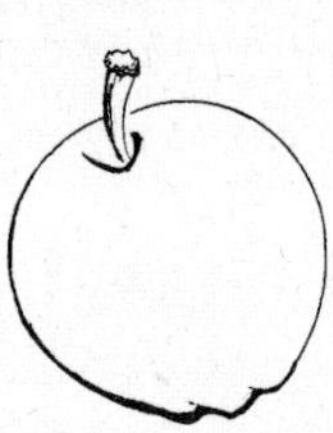

Underline the word that matches the picture.

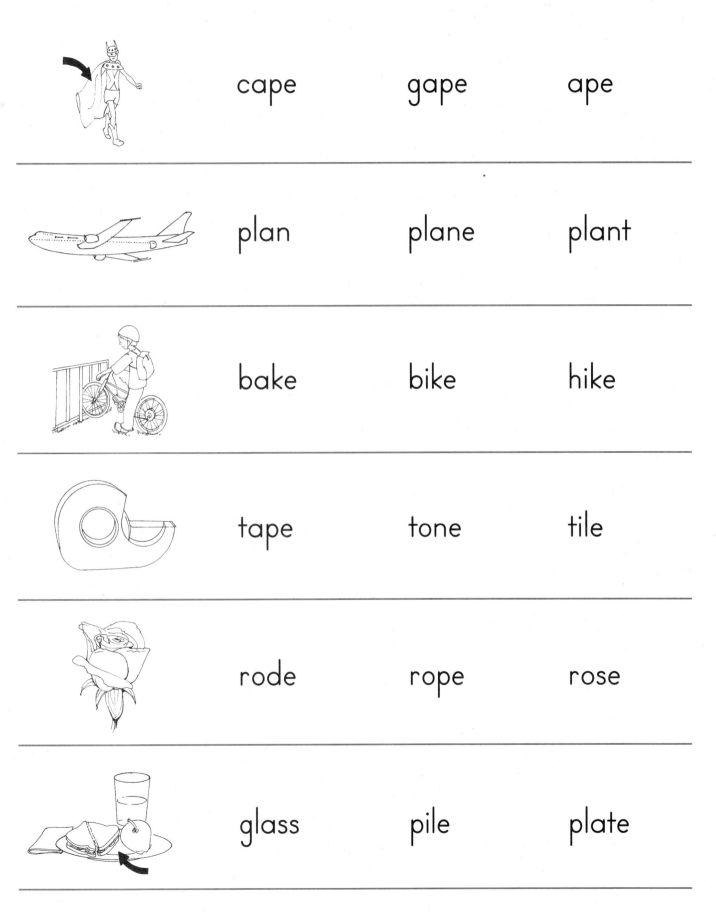

	cape	gape	ape
	plan	plane	plant
	bake	bike	hike
	tape	tone	tile
	rode	rope	rose
	glass	pile	plate

Fill in each blank with a word from the box, then read the sentence.

skate	plate	fire
cone	drove	face

Steve will get a _____ for Jane.

Mom _____ the van.

Take that _____ to the rink.

A _____ will make smoke.

Chad had a smile on his_____

Her lunch is on that _____.

Check the sentence that matches the picture.

☐ Ted did wave to Pam.

☐ Pam can fix a flat tire.

☐ The rose is for Mom.

☐ The tot did gaze at the cone.

☐ Jake did tell a joke.

☐ Jake is an umpire.

☐ The game will last a long time.

☐ The rule says not to jump on the bunk.

☐ The name of this kid is Pete.

☐ Pete is the name of his pet snake.

☐ Cash is in the safe.

☐ This shape is a cube.

11

Lesson 45

Magic e in two-syllable words

Say the names of the pictures. Then circle the pictures whose names have the same vowel sound in the second syllable.

Say the names of all the pictures you circled. What is the same about the vowel sounds in the second syllables of these names?

Read the word and circle the matching picture. Listen for the vowel that says its name.

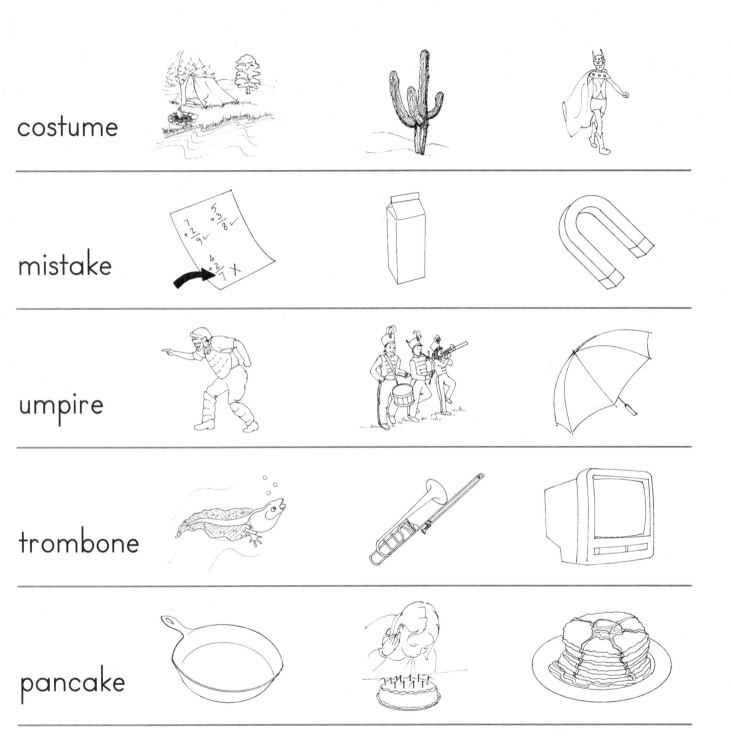

costume

mistake

umpire

trombone

pancake

Underline the word that matches the picture.

empire	umpire	uphill
bagpipe	bag	trombone
crust	costume	classmate
drum	trombone	basket
pan	pancake	cake

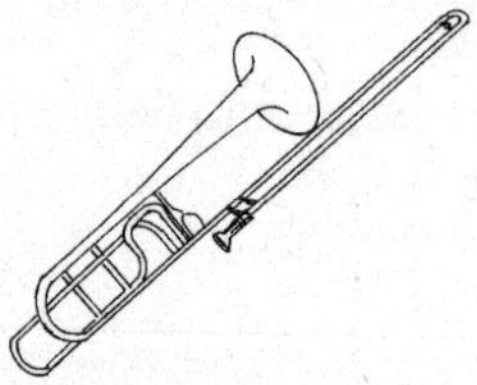

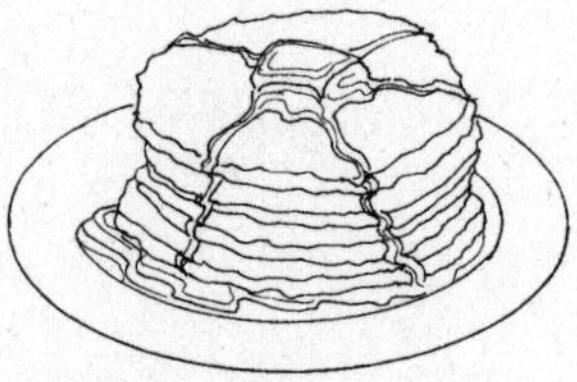

14

Fill in each blank with a word from the box, then read the sentence.

---

compute	mistake	costume
trombone	umpire	

This _____ was at the ball game.

His _____ did include a cape.

A _____ will complete the band.

He made a _____ on his math quiz.

I can _____ my grade for this

class.

Check the sentence that matches the picture.

☐ I like this costume.

☐ Len can compute the math problem.

☐ Jon made a mistake.

☐ Her tent is at the campsite.

☐ Mom will confine Bill to his bed.

☐ Sam likes the trombone.

☐ My bike helmet is big.

☐ I like pancakes.

☐ The sunshine fell on John.

☐ The tadpole fell on Jane.

☐ Did the bandit escape?

☐ He is an umpire.

16

Read the story, then draw a picture that answers the question at the end.

The Band

It is time to line up a band for the contest. Bill can play his trombone, and Jess will play the bagpipes. Kate has a trumpet and a bell. Mike has a snare drum and drumsticks. To be a complete band they must have five. Who can they invite to help them win the contest?

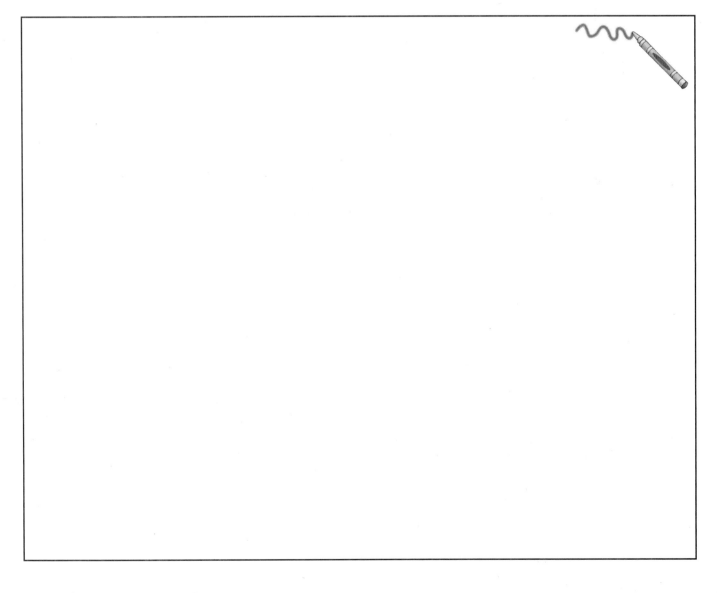

Lesson 46

ph as /f/

ph says /f/ as in  **phone.**

Read the word and circle the picture it names.

graph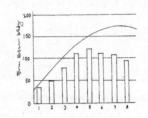

pamphlet

Ralph

phone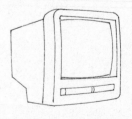

Phil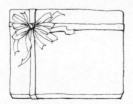

Write the word under the picture.

| elephant | graph | Phil |
| phone | pamphlet | |

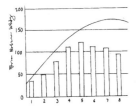

_____

_____

_____

_____

_____

Fill in each blank with a word from the box, then read the sentence.

Ralph	phonics	pamphlet
graph	phone	

This _____ is fun to look at.

_____ is in a costume for the play.

In math she did use a _____.

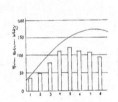

Sal did chat on the _____.

Use _____ to help you spell.

Check the sentence that matches the picture.

☐ This is a saxophone.

☐ See the big trunk and tusk on that elephant!

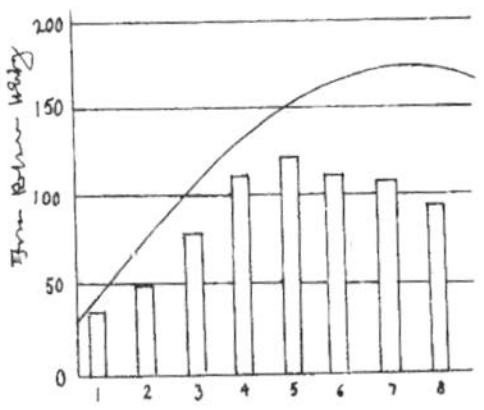

☐ A graph can help the class.

☐ The campsite is full.

☐ The phone did ring.

☐ Phil is late.

☐ Ralph is a tadpole.

☐ Ralph is inside his house.

21

Read the story, and draw a picture of what the pig ate.

Ralph and His Pig

Ralph has a pet pig. The pig ate a pamphlet, a phone, and a bit of cash. Ralph made a graph of all his pet ate. What was on his graph?

Lesson 47

ck as /k/

ck says /k/ as in duck.

Say the names of the pictures. Then circle the picture whose name ends with /k/.

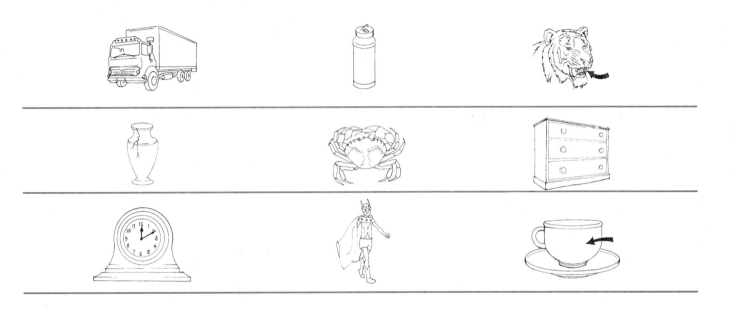

Say the names of the pictures. Then circle the picture whose name has the sound /k/ in the middle.

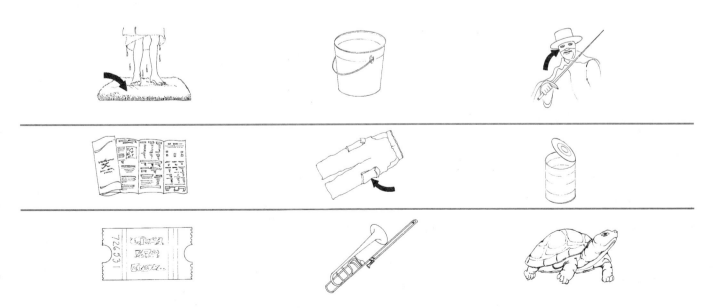

Underline the word that matches the picture.

	truck	trunk	tuck
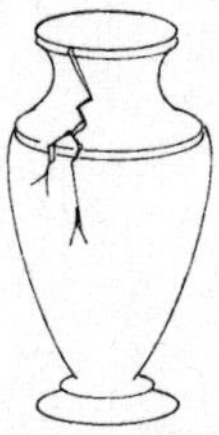	rock	stock	crack
	block	black	blink
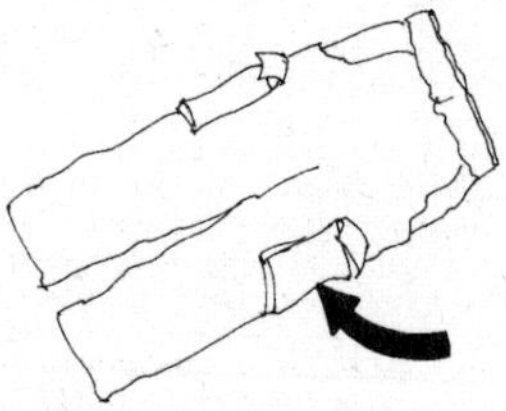	picket	pocket	puppet
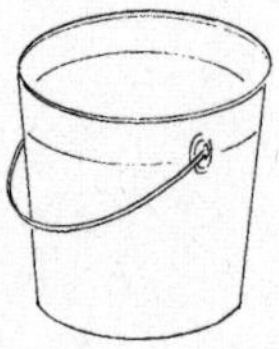	bucket	basket	bracket
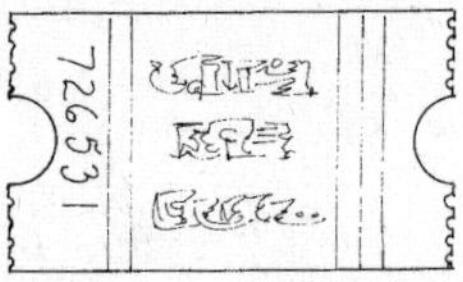	tick-tock	ticket	trombone

24

Take off the last letter of each word, and replace it with ck. Then write and say the new word.

blob   _____

tan   _____

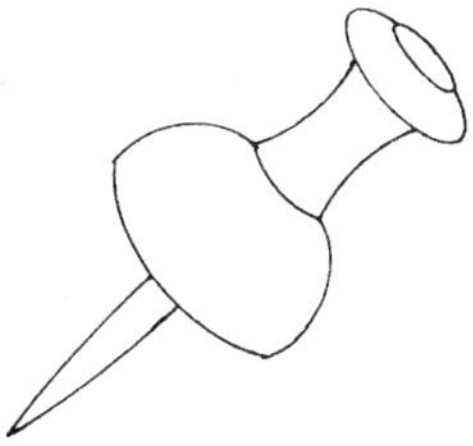

pan   _____

dug   _____

strum   _____

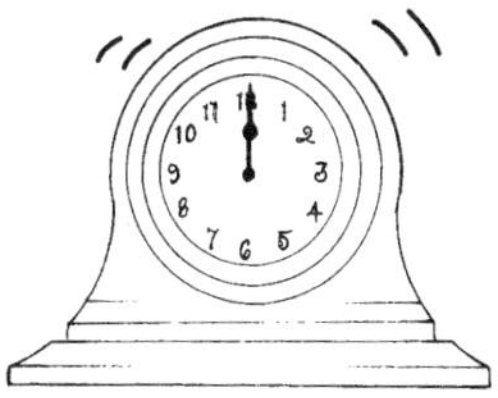

bad   _____

Fill in each blank with a word from the box, then read the sentence.

snack	tick-tock	pocket
puck	ticket	bucket

Buck had a _____ to the play.

The clock went _____ .

I had a _____ and late lunch.

Bring her skates and _____ to

the rink.

Fill the _____ with fish.

She had a sock in her back _____ .

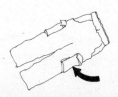

Check the sentence that matches the picture.

☐	A big rock is in the pond.
☐	A duck is in the pond.

☐	The chick did cluck.
☐	The clock struck six.

☐	Ted is at the bike rack.
☐	Scrub his back.

☐	The tot did play with a block.
☐	The tablet is blank.

☐	Tam had no luck.
☐	Yum! Sam did lick the cone.

☐	A rocket is fast.
☐	Her pocket is full.

Read the phrases and draw a picture of one of them.

a duck that quacks

a backpack strap

a quick reptile

a clock that struck ten

a bike rack at a bus stop

Lesson 48

ea as /ē/

Say the names of the pictures. Then circle the pictures whose names have the same vowel sound.

Say the names of the pictures you circled. What vowel sound do you hear?

ea says /ē/ as in leaf.

Read the word and circle the picture it names.

beach

leaf

wheat

tear

team

meal

Underline the word that matches the picture.

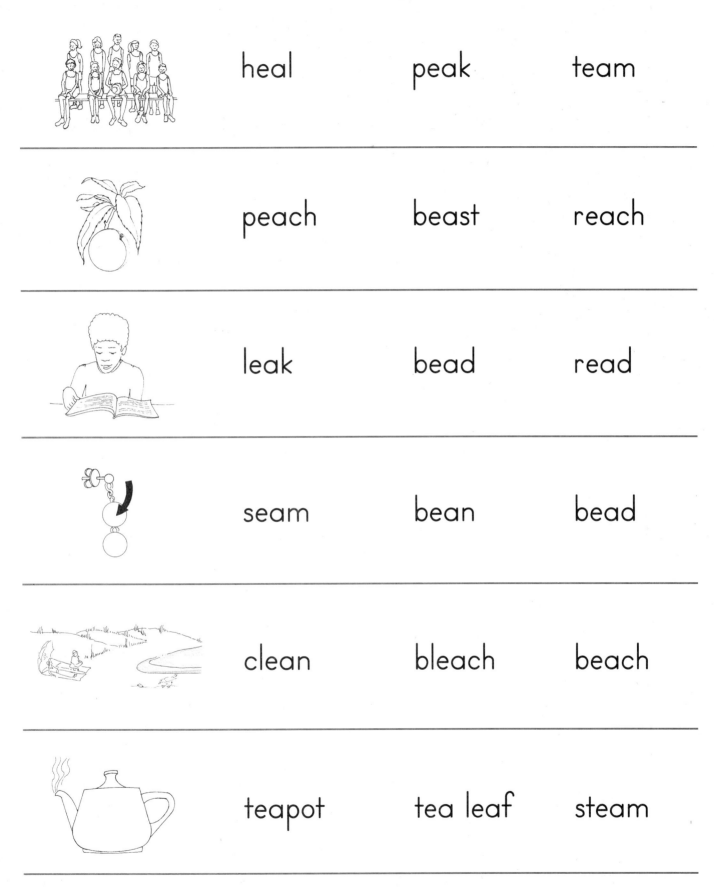

heal	peak	team
peach	beast	reach
leak	bead	read
seam	bean	bead
clean	bleach	beach
teapot	tea leaf	steam

31

Write the word under the picture.

beach	leaf	read
steam	peach	earring

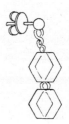

_____

_____

_____

_____

_____

_____

Check the sentence that matches the picture.

☐	The peach is ripe.
☐	The peak is in the east.

☐	Jen ran a mile on the track.
☐	Lunch is the best meal!

☐	She can teach math.
☐	The teapot is hot.

☐	It is fun to swim at the beach.
☐	The bleach did stink.

☐	Yeast will help it rise.
☐	A year is a long time.

☐	Jean is the teammate of Steve.
☐	Ted is at the seashore.

Read the story, then draw a picture from it.

The Dream

Dean had a dream that he was on a beach. A gull did peck at the sand near the seat where Dean sat. In this dream he could hear the gull speak! It made Dean leap from his seat. Then the gull gave a squeak in his ear and crept to the sea. It was just a dream but felt real to Dean!

Lesson 49

oa as /ō/

Say the names of the pictures. Then circle the pictures whose names have the same vowel sound.

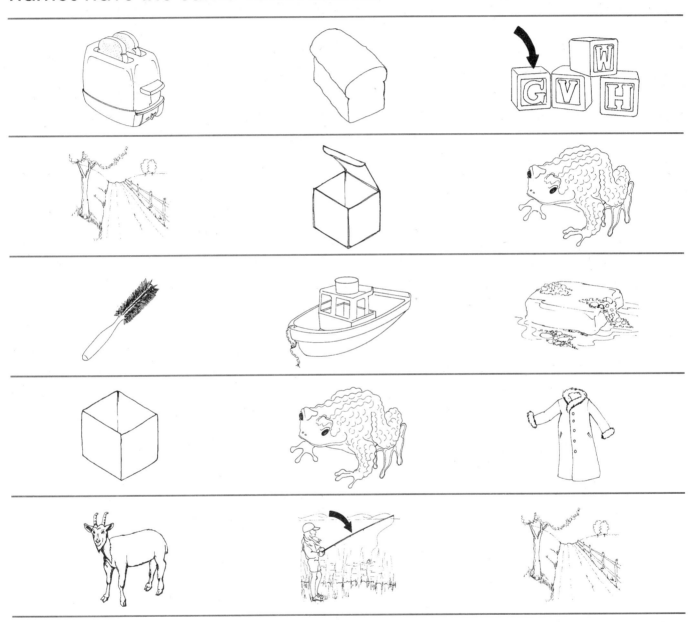

Say the names of the pictures you circled. What vowel sound do you hear?

oa says /ō/ as in **soap.**

Read the word and circle the picture it names.

goat

toast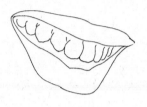

toad

loaf

road

steamboat

Underline the word that matches the picture.

 moan	foam	road
 coast	toast	soap
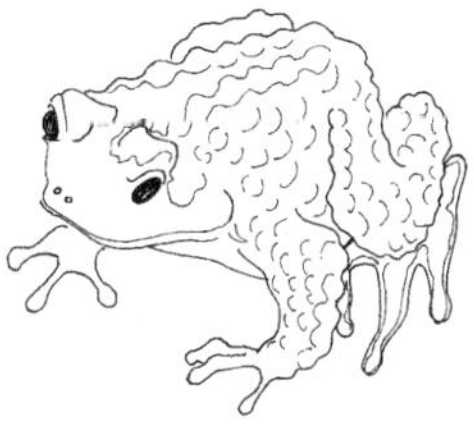 soak	toad	loan
 coast	coat	code
 bloat	steamboat	oatmeal

Write the word under the picture.

goat	toast	loaf
coat	road	soap

_____

_____

_____

_____

_____

_____

Fill in each blank with a word from the box, then read the sentence.

croak	steamboat	loaf
goat	road	float

The _____ did float.

The toad will boast with a big _____.

Shall we hike on the path, or drive on the

_____?

Did you bake that _____ at home?

The _____ did bleat.

The soap will not sink, it does _____.

Check the sentence that matches the picture.

- [ ] The road is long.
- [ ] A toad sits at the crossroads.

- [ ] Wet soap will slip.
- [ ] Do not approach the steamboat.

- [ ] A toad will croak.
- [ ] The men will load the van

- [ ] My throat is sore.
- [ ] Save the toast and oatmeal.

- [ ] Sam soaked in the bathtub.
- [ ] Did Sal like to boast?

- [ ] An oak is at the campsite.
- [ ] The dog roamed from his home.

Lesson 50

ai as /ā/

Say the names of the pictures. Then circle the pictures whose names have the same vowel sound.

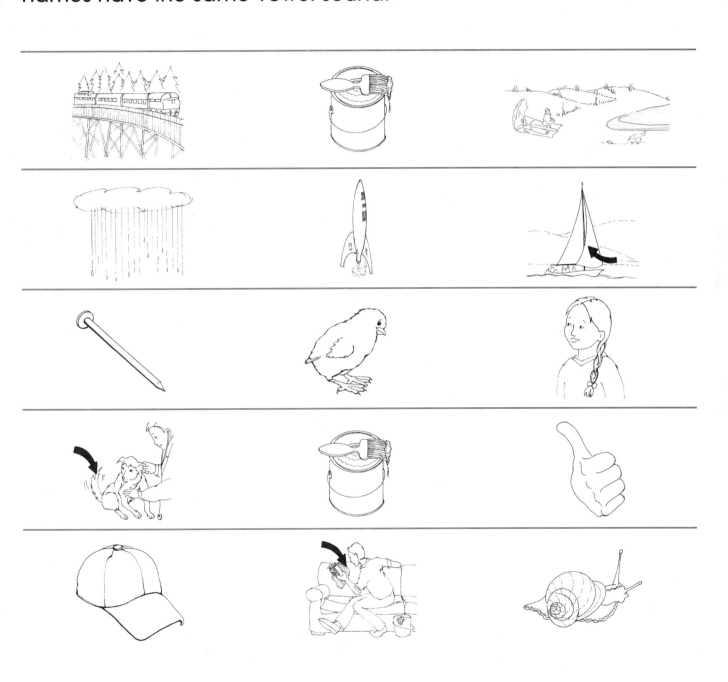

Say the names of the pictures you circled. What vowel sound do you hear?

ai says /ā/as in **paint.**

Read the word and circle the picture it names.

stain

train

snail

sail

paint
 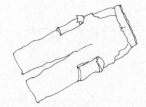 

mailbox
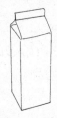 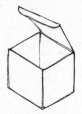 

ai says /ā/as in **paint.**

Underline the word that matches the picture.

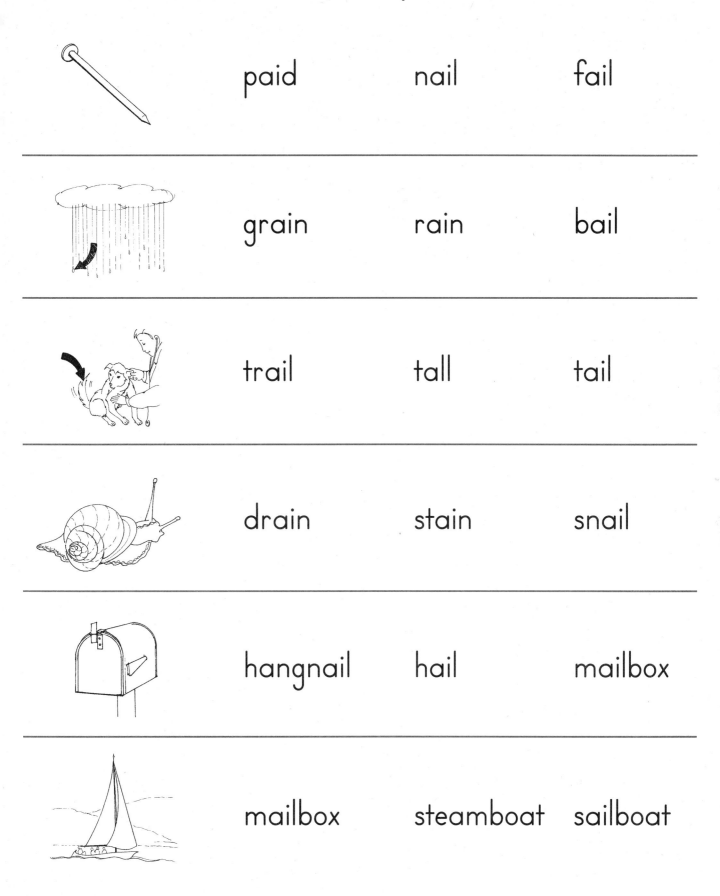

	paid	nail	fail
	grain	rain	bail
	trail	tall	tail
	drain	stain	snail
	hangnail	hail	mailbox
	mailbox	steamboat	sailboat

43

Write the word under the picture.

nail	mailbox	sailboat
snail	paint	train

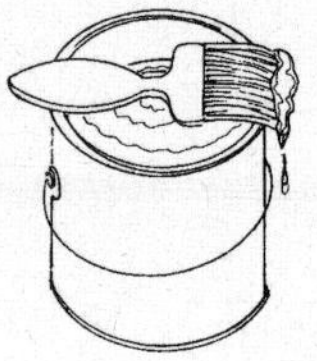

_____

_____

_____

_____

_____

_____

Fill in each blank with a word from the box, then read the sentence.

mailbox	Raindrops	air
sailboat	braid	train

_____ fell before the hail.

Her hair is in a _____.

The _____ is late.

The _____ is by the steamship.

Put stamps on the mail in the _____.

The _____ is fresh and clean.

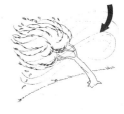

Check the sentence that matches the picture.

☐ Did he sprain his hand?

☐ Did he scrub the stain?

☐ The pail did contain fish.

☐ The paint is wet.

☐ This snail has a thick shell.

☐ The air is fresh.

☐ The tail is long.

☐ The tile is strong.

☐ The rain did not stop.

☐ That is a sailboat.

☐ Mike and Jean hike on the trail.

☐ Jon and Beth ride the train.

Lesson 51

e as /ē/

Say the names of the pictures. Then circle the pictures whose names have the same vowel sound.

Say the names of the pictures you circled. What vowel sound do you hear?

ee says /ē/ as in 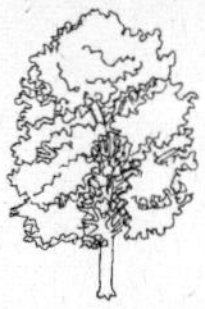 **tree.**

Read the word and circle the picture it names.

sleep

eel

teeth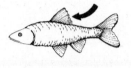

sheep

queen

beehive

 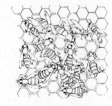 

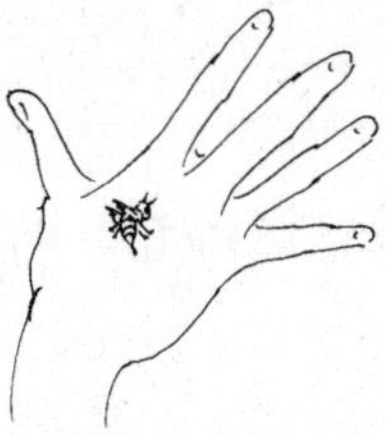

48

Underline the word that matches the picture.

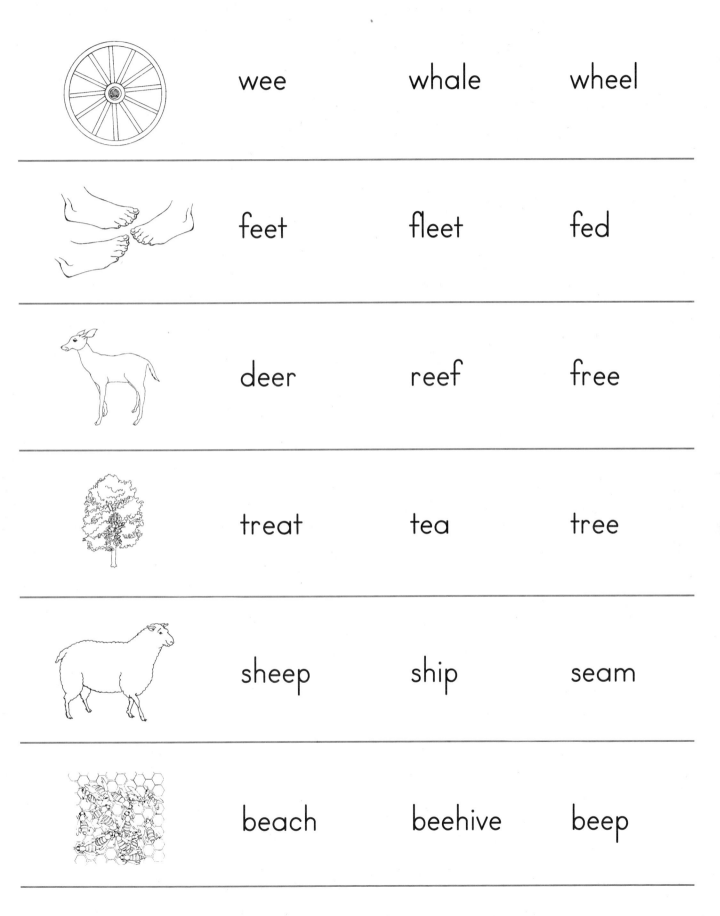

(wheel)	wee	whale	wheel
(feet)	feet	fleet	fed
(deer)	deer	reef	free
(tree)	treat	tea	tree
(sheep)	sheep	ship	seam
(beehive)	beach	beehive	beep

49

Fill in each blank with a word from the box, then read the sentence.

Peep	seek	sweep
fee	sheep	treetop

It is fun to play hide and _____.

His _____ was paid in cash.

The chick said, "_____".

His task is to _____ the path.

The _____ did eat green grass.

A raindrop fell on the _____.

Check the sentence that matches the picture.

☐	Would you like to eat a beet?
☐	Do not feed the sheep.

☐	Make a beeline for the steep hill.
☐	The dog will sleep.

☐	The bees make a hive.
☐	Water the plant seed.

☐	The tot did screech.
☐	The screen is wide.

☐	Peel the skin off that grape.
☐	Do not peek in the gift box.

☐	The jeep is green.
☐	Jim gave a speech in class.

51

Read the phrases and draw a picture of one of them.

a steep hill

the deep sea

a cat stuck in a tree

a bike with big wheels

the feet of a queen

Lesson 52

ay as /ā/

Say the names of the pictures. Then circle the pictures whose names have the same vowel sound at the end.

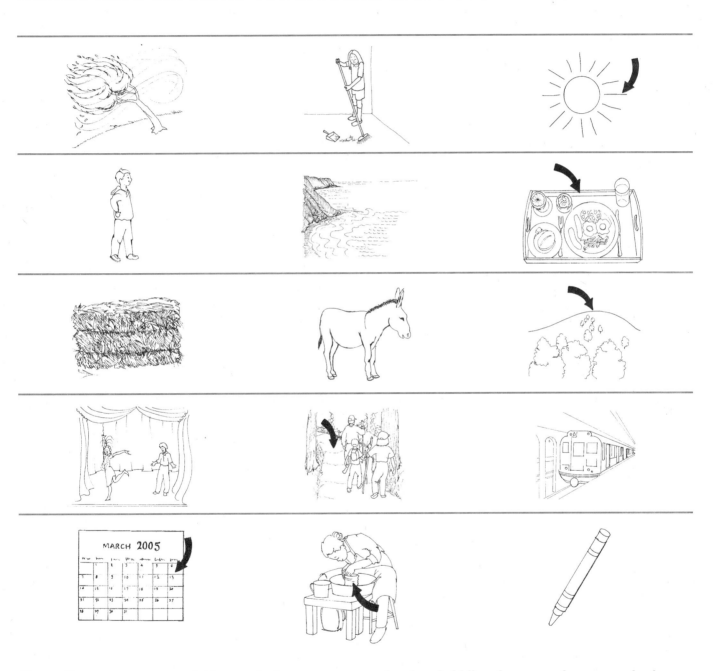

Say the names of the pictures you circled. What vowel sound do you hear at the end?

ay says /ā/ as in **tray.**

Read the word and circle the picture it names.

clay

tray

ray

hay

subway

Underline the word that matches the picture.

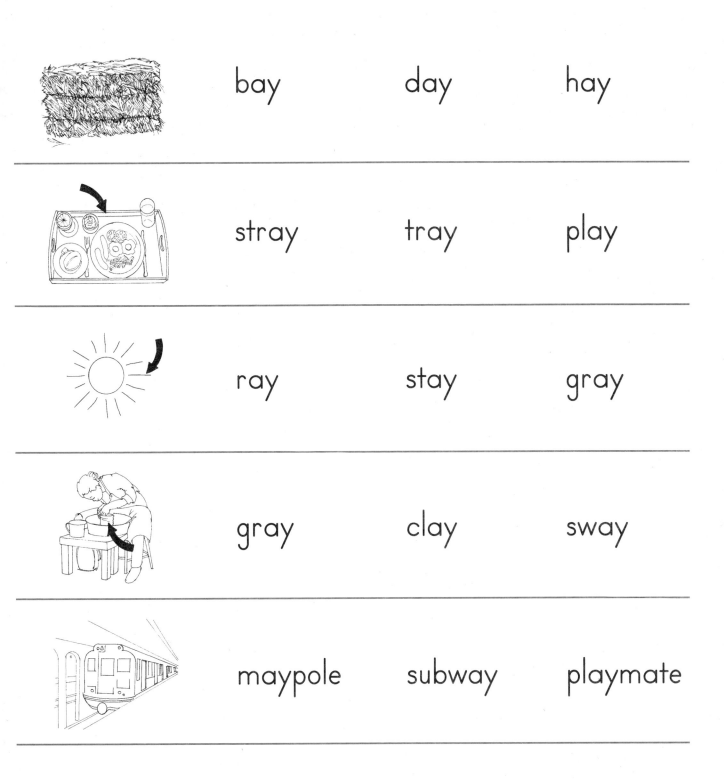

bay	day	hay
stray	tray	play
ray	stay	gray
gray	clay	sway
maypole	subway	playmate

55

Write the word under the picture.

subway	hay	day
bay	tray	

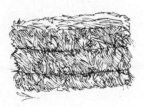

_____   _____   _____

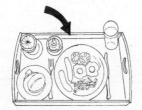

_____   _____

Fill in each blank with a word from the box, then read the sentence.

bay	play	clay
hay	tray	subway

Set the glass on that _____.

The _____ can go fast.

Pile the _____ at the pigpen.

We went to see a _____.

A cliff is near the _____.

Jen made that _____ pot.

Check the sentence that matches the picture.

The stray dog said, "Woof."

Do not stay too long.

Do you like to sail in the bay?

The beast did bray.

Lunch is on the tray.

The tree did sway in the wind.

Was the shirt on display?

The hay did smell fresh.

How fast is this subway?

Is the jeep tire flat?

The clay is in a lump.

The crayon is made of wax.

Lesson 53

oe as /ō/

Say the names of the pictures. Then circle the pictures whose names have the same vowel sound.

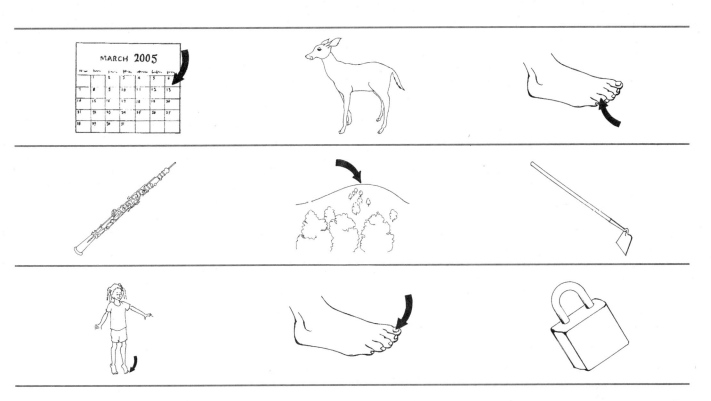

Say the names of the pictures you circled. What vowel sound do you hear in all of them?

oe says /ō/ as in 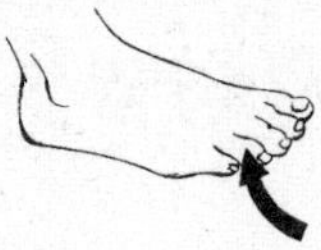 **toe.**

Read the word and circle the picture it names.

toe

doe

Joe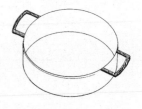

hoe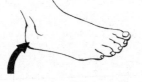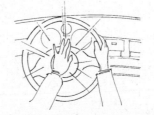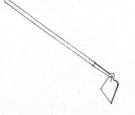

tiptoe

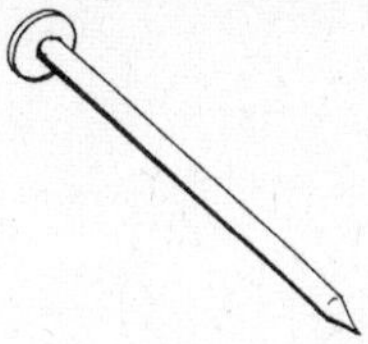

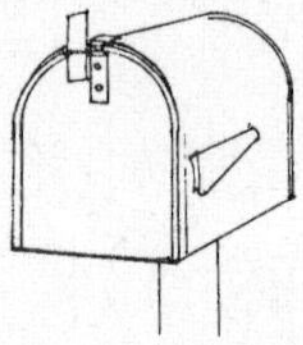

toenail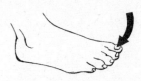

Underline the word that matches the picture.

oak	toe	oat
Joe	joke	jacket
tiptoe	maypole	sock
doe	doll	dog
ax	hem	hoe
feet	finger	toenail

Fill in each blank with a word from the box, then read the sentence.

oboe	toenail	hoe
doe	toe	

Moe plays the _____ in the band.

Did Ren stub his _____?

You can paint her _____ red.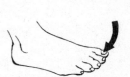

Kathleen dug with her garden _____.

The _____ ran past the campsite.

Check the sentence that matches the picture.

☐ Jane got up on tiptoe.

☐ The bandit did tiptoe down the street.

☐ This is an oboe.

☐ Woe is me!

☐ Dad had a hoe to weed the garden.

☐ Jean is mad at Mike, her foe.

☐ The toenail is long.

☐ The tonsil is red.

☐ Jill hangs from a tree.

☐ Joe is under the tree.

Lesson 54

Syllable Division Review

Draw a line to divide between the syllables. Underline the vowels and circle the consonants. Then read the word.

mailbox	oatmeal
beehive	playpen
coffee	subway
steamboat	pilot
toenail	magnet
banjo	crayon

Read the word and circle the picture it names.

steamboat

mailbox

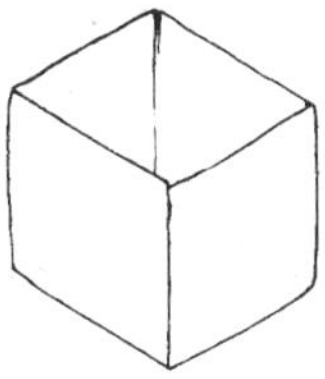

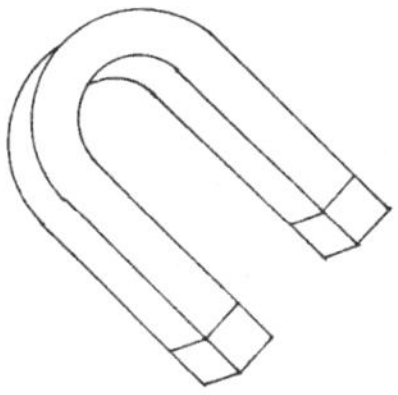

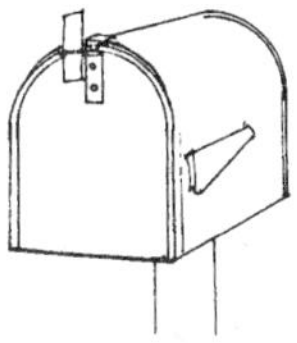

pamphlet

subway

tiptoe

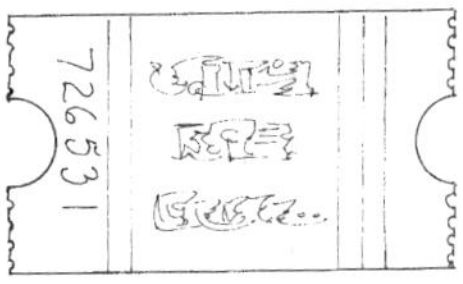

banjo

Underline the word that matches the picture.

toenail	tiptoe	ticket
doe	oboe	loaf
umpire	empire	earring
packet	pocket	pancake
peach	pamphlet	airplane
tadpole	tiptoe	teapot

Fill in each blank with a word from the box, then read the sentence.

tiptoe	seamstress	combine
oboe	dispute	subway

A _____ could mend the rip in the pants.

I will invite Stan to play his _____.

On _____, Kathleen snuck up on Joe.

To bake a coffee cake, _____ milk with yeast.

Rose had a _____ with her playmates.

Mom can take the _____ to her job.

Check the sentence that matches the picture.

☐ The pancakes are hot.

☐ The muffin is sweet.

☐ Did you see the display?

☐ On Sunday we saw a play.

☐ The pilot is in the airplane.

☐ The pilot had a green plant.

☐ I like oatmeal with toast.

☐ Jane played her oboe in the band.

☐ I saw steam escape from the teapot.

☐ My toenail has a bit of seaweed on it.

☐ The red crayon is missing from the box.

☐ It is fun to sculpt with clay.

Read the story, then draw a picture from it.

The Crayon

It was playtime, but Wayne's playmate was not home. So Wayne made a beeline to his best plaything: a green crayon. With that crayon he made a beehive with three bees, a teapot on the stove, the ear of a peacock, and a steamboat on the bay. Wayne's mom looked at what he made.

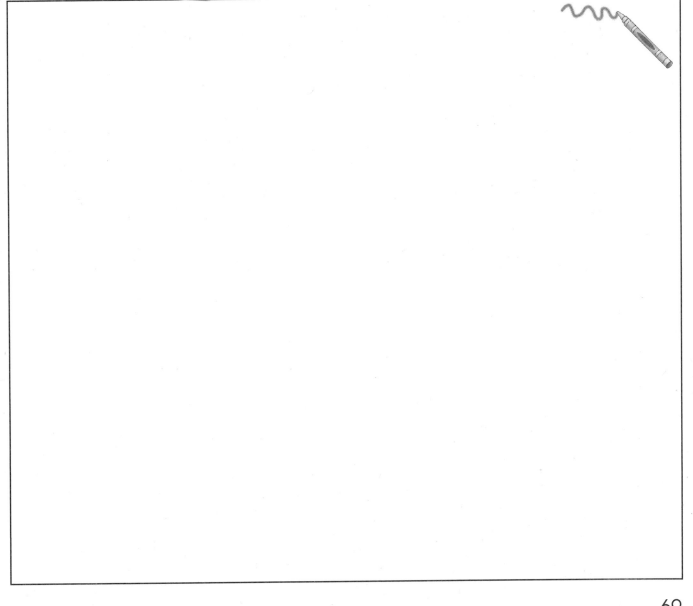

Lesson 55

Review of the spellings for /k/

1. Use k after a long vowel before silent e, as in **lake.**

2. Use k after two vowels, as in **beak, or** **oak.**

3. Use k after a consonant, as in **bank.**

4. Use ck after a short vowel, as in **back.**

Fill in the blank with k, ke, or ck to complete the words. Then write the number of the rule you used.

sti _____ # _____

mil _____ # _____

soa _____ # _____

ca _____ # _____

bi _____ # _____

Write the word under the picture.

beak	rack	milk
tank	skate	soak

_____

_____

_____

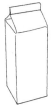

_____

_____

_____

71

Fill in each blank with a word from the box, then read the sentence.

bunk	read	ticket
blocks	snake	leak

Jack played with his _____.

This pamphlet is fun to _____.

The _____ did hiss.

Can you sleep on that _____ bed?

You need a _____ to see the play.

The boat sprung a _____.

Check the sentence that matches the picture.

- [ ] Yum! We can share that cake.

- [ ] Lick that cone before it drips.

- [ ] The duck did quack, then shut his beak.

- [ ] A snake can be quick.

- [ ] Do not eat a snack before lunch.

- [ ] That stack of pancakes is for you.

- [ ] Lock your bike on the bike rack.

- [ ] Bring your skates and puck to the rink.

- [ ] A cop did stop the bandit before he could rob the bank.

- [ ] The bandit hid his face benind a mask.

73

Read the story, then draw a picture about it.

Mike and His Bike

Mike was at the bike rack. The air in his tires had leaked, and he saw that the back tire was flat. What bad luck! Just then, Tess came past on her bike. She had a spare tube for the tire in her backpack. Tess and Mike fixed the tire, then went for a bike ride.

Mike's tire squeaked, but it did not leak!

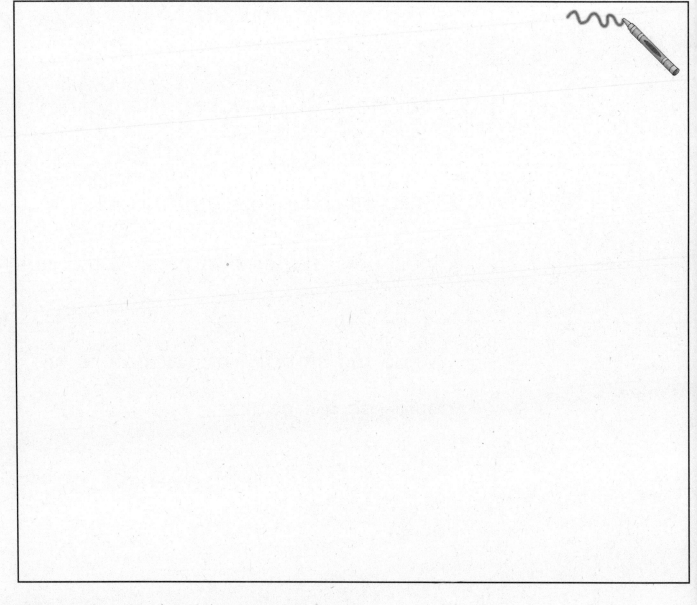